SINK YOUR TEETH INTO
DRAGONS

L. J. TRACOSAS

Dragon Bestiary

THAR BE DRAGONS—EVERYWHERE!

Images of dragons as fierce, fire-breathing creatures that fly around and terrorize castles are popular subjects for books, movies, and TV shows. These dragon stories are common in Europe and other countries in the Western Hemisphere. But dragon lore can be found all over the world—from the frozen landscapes of Scandinavia to the deserts of Africa to the waterways of Southeast Asia.

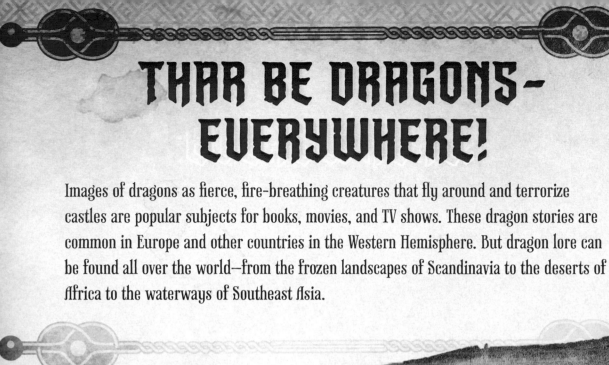

Dragon Attitude

Not all dragons are evil monsters that terrorize villages. Many dragons in Western culture—mostly those from Europe—have bad reputations. At the very least, they cause mischief; at their worst they are responsible for death and destruction. But not all dragons are so terrible! In many Eastern cultures—in Asia and India, for example—dragons are kind creatures that bring wealth, good crops, and water. Some also protect important people and places.

CREATURE FEATURES

What do dragons look like? There's a lot of variety in the dragon world! While many dragons have unique characteristics, here are a few that many—but not all—dragons share:

Sssnake-like body

The word *dragon* comes from the Greek and Latin words for *serpent*. Nearly every dragon in these pages has a serpent's body or tail.

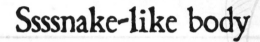

Wings: Not every dragon has wings—and even those that do have wings don't necessarily fly. Many dragons have bat-like wings that are extended bones with a leathery skin flap forming the wing.

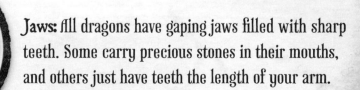

Jaws: All dragons have gaping jaws filled with sharp teeth. Some carry precious stones in their mouths, and others just have teeth the length of your arm.

Were Dragons Real?

It's a wonder how universal dragon lore is. So many cultures have stories of dragons or dragon-like creatures. Could dragons have been real? Some scientists, historians, and mythology experts think these real-life animals could have inspired dragon stories:

Dinosaurs: People have known about dinosaurs—or at least their huge fossils—since about the 4th century BC. It's possible that a pteranadon's skeleton could have been the inspiration for a winged monster, or a T. rex fossil was confused for a dragon's.

Large reptiles: Reptiles like the Nile Crocodile or monitor lizards could account for some dragon stories. Crocodiles lurk in riverbanks and stay mostly hidden underwater while hunting, exposing just their eyes and snout, leaving the rest of their body up to the imagination.

Huge snakes: Serpents figure so heavily in the descriptions of dragons, it's possible that tales of huge snakes similar to today's anacondas or reticulated pythons could account for dragon tales.

Whales: These truly giant creatures have inspired countless tales among fishermen. But washed ashore, their bones could resemble that of a giant dragon-like beast.

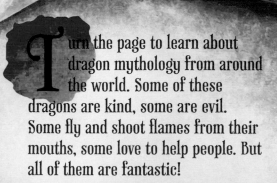

Turn the page to learn about dragon mythology from around the world. Some of these dragons are kind, some are evil. Some fly and shoot flames from their mouths, some love to help people. But all of them are fantastic!

EUROPEAN DRAGON

Knight Terror

According to legend, European dragons could be found in mountain ranges from England to Germany about a thousand years ago. With their massive, scaly bodies; fire breath; and habit of hoarding gold, they are the real stars of the stories about knights rescuing princesses.

Region: Western Europe
Time Period: 5th–15th centuries
Habitat: Mountain caves
Flight Capable: Yes
Fire Breath: Yes

Some people believe these dragons spoke their own language and could even communicate with humans.

Dragon Bite Note #1:

European Dragons were carnivores, meaning they ate meat. They had strong teeth with jaws stretching wide enough that they could snap up goats, sheep, and even cows.

LONG

Chinese Dragon (LONG)

Good Luck

Here's one dragon you'd be happy to see! Long, also known as Lung or the Chinese dragon, was a kind and generous creature. Instead of bringing terror, Long brought good luck and heavenly bounty. There were different types of Long; some ruled the earth, and some ruled the sea and skies.

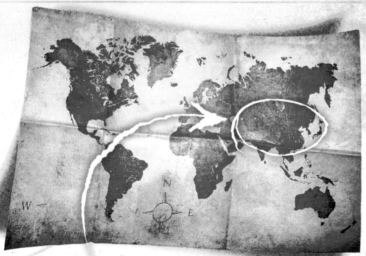

Region: China
Time Period: 30th century BC
Habitat: Waterways, like rivers and lakes
Flight Capable: Yes
Fire Breath: Yes

Even though this dragon was kind, Long was still powerful. With fire breath and four legs that each ended in a five-clawed foot, it was fortunate that Long brought good luck!

Dragon Bite Note #2:

Long's mouth was filled with sharp, thick, and curved teeth—and also a pearl. The pearl symbolized wisdom.

ZMEY GORNYNYCH

Slavic Dragon (zah-MAY GOR-neh-nitch)

Three Heads Are Better Than One

Zmey Gornynych was a terrible sight: It had not one, but three snapping, snarling heads. It was able to walk upright on its strong back legs. Zmey Gornynych had magical powers, which it used to create chaos and to kidnap people. This is one dragon you don't want to mess with.

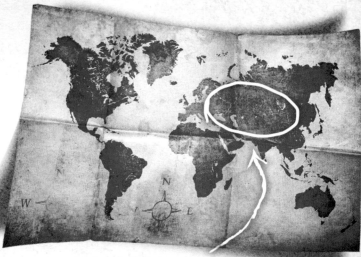

Region: Russia, Eastern Europe
Time Period: Unknown
Habitat: Castles filled with riches
Flight Capable: Yes
Fire Breath: Yes

Zmey Gornynych is also know as Zmei Gorynich, and is sometimes described as being half human and half serpent.

Dragon Bite Note #3:

With its three snapping jaws full of pointy teeth, Zmey Gornynych was a top predator. Each mouth had two long fangs, perfect for snaring prey.

GARGOUILLE

French dragon (gar-GOO-ee)

Watery Wrecker

Gargouille was a monster that terrorized fishermen along the river Seine in France. This huge dragon could whip up waterspouts—which are waterborne tornadoes—using its four legs and four wings. It would flip over fishing boats and sometimes gobble up their crews. Legend has it that a priest was able to finally stop Gargouille's terror simply by making the sign of the cross.

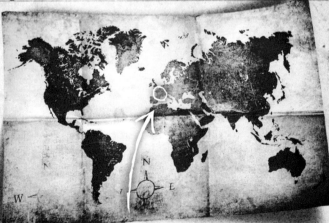

Region: Europe (Northeastern France)
Time Period: 12th century or earlier
Habitat: Waterways, like rivers and lakes
Flight Capable: Yes
Fire Breath: Yes

Some say Gargouille was the inspiration for gargoyles, the sculpted spouts that spit water away from cathedrals. The sculptures often depict horrifying monsters and goblins.

Dragon Bite Note #4:

Gargouille had a beak-like jaw filled with jagged upper and lower teeth that fit together almost like a zipper.

ETHIOPIAN DRAGON

An Elephant-Sized Appetite

Ethiopian dragons were enormous creatures that lived in eastern Africa. According to legend, Ethiopian dragons had magical stones in their skulls called Draconitas. For the Draconitas to keep their power, they had to be taken out of dragons while the creatures were still alive. The best way to do this? Lull the dragon to sleep with special herbs first.

Region: Eastern Africa
Time Period: Unknown
Habitat: Dry deserts
Flight Capable: Yes
Fire Breath: Unknown

When their food source was scarce, Ethiopian dragons could wrap themselves together and float across the sea in search of more food.

Dragon Bite Note #5:

Ethiopian Dragons hunted elephants, so they had to have very strong, thick teeth to first grab and then rip through prey.

KNUCKER

(NUH-kur)

Nasty Knuckers

Knuckers were wicked water dragons. They lived in knuckerholes, almost perfectly round woodland waterholes fed by underground springs that kept them at a constant temperature year-round. Legend has it that one of the most wicked Knuckers was slayed by pie! The poisoned pie was delivered by a horse pulling a cart—which the Knucker ate too! The poison did its job quickly.

Region: Britain
Time Period: 8th–11th centuries
Habitat: Knuckerholes
Flight Capable: No
Fire Breath: No

Knuckers did not fly—they preferred to lurk in dark, wet places—but they did have very small wings, which suggest that they may have flown at one time.

Dragon Bite Note #6:

Knuckers terrorized nearby villages by stealing people's things, and gobbling up sheep and other livestock. Their teeth were inward-curving in order to snare fleeing victims.

IMUGI

(ee-MOO-gee)

Maybe Dragons

Imugis looked like huge serpents with python-like bodies. They lived in dark and wet places. Despite their creepy appearance, they were thought to be kind and to deliver good luck. Some people believe Imugi were "protodragons"—meaning creatures that would eventually become dragons, if they survived for 1,000 years.

Region: Asia (Korea)
Time Period: Unknown
Habitat: Rivers, lakes, and oceans
Flight Capable: No
Fire Breath: No

Imugis are kind creatures known to help people, even if it meant harm to themselves. In one story, an Imugi defied the gods and brought rain to some much-needed crops.

Dragon Bite Note #7:

Imugis very closely resembled snakes, so their large front fangs and forked tongue will look familiar.

AMPHIPTERE

(am-FIP-teer)

Flying Pythons!

Amphipteres looked like huge snakes with great bat wings and a spiked, arrow-tipped tail. These beasts terrorized villagers in medieval Europe. Amphipteres were known for their nasty natures, swooping in to scare people and snatch up livestock. They lived in forests and preferred to be alone—when not attacking people, that is.

Region: Europe
Time Period: 16th century or before
Habitat: Woodlands
Flight Capable: Yes
Fire Breath: Unknown

You can find Amphipteres in many coats of arms, which are symbols that show history and information about a family. In a person's coat of arms, the Amphiptere was a sign of that family being fierce.

Dragon Bite Note #8:

Amphipteres had short, crocodile-like snouts. Also like a crocodile, they had smooth pointed teeth designed to snag prey, which was very useful for airborne attacks.

NĀGA

(NAH-gah)

The Mysterious Nāga

People have reported Nâga sightings throughout Asia, and each description is a little bit different. According to various legends, Nāgas could have anywhere from one to five heads. The five-headed kind guarded temples in Indonesia and Thailand. Still other cultures in Malaysia describe Nāgas as monstrous evil creatures that lived in the sea and terrorized fishermen.

Region: Southeast Asia (Indonesia, Thailand, Malaysia, the Philippines)
Time Period: Unknown
Habitat: Oceans and waterways
Flight Capable: Unknown
Fire Breath: Unknown

Nāga means different things in different cultures. For example, the Nāgas in Indian folklore are human-snake hybrids, people from the waist up and serpents from the waist down.

Dragon Bite Note #9:

To guard important places and scare away intruders, Nāgas needed to look tough. And they did, especially thanks to their double set of upper teeth.

WYVERN

(WHY-vern)

Upright Rascals

Wyverns had a snake-like body, bat-like wings, a barbed tail, and two hind legs that allowed them to stand upright. Like Amphipteres, they were mean and ruthless creatures, attacking villages to create fear. Wyverns are considered "lesser dragons," or dragon-like creatures because they had only two legs and usually could not breathe fire.

Region: Europe
Time Period: Early 17th century
Habitat: Woodlands near villages
Flight Capable: Yes
Fire Breath: Sometimes

There is a species of Wyvern known as the Sea-Wyvern, which had a fish's body, lurked in the depths of the oceans, and attacked ships.

Dragon Bite Note #10:

Wyverns had jagged, serrated teeth for sawing and ripping. They were often shown with barbed wingtips, which they used for slashing and grabbing.

HYDRA

(HI-drah)

How Many Heads?

Behold the Hydra! This beast was a star of Greek myths. Hydra lurked in Lerna, a lake that was one entryway to the Underworld. This creature had poisonous blood and gave off deadly fumes. Its most interesting feature was that the Hydra had anywhere from six or more heads, because if one was cut off, multiple heads would sprout in its place.

Region: Mediterranean
Time Period: 8th~6th century BC
Habitat: The swamp outside Lake Lerna
Flight Capable: No
Fire Breath: No

Hydra was the offspring of Echidna and Typhon, who gave birth to many mythical monsters, including the Chimera.

Dragon Bite Note #11:

Hydra had too many teeth to count! Its teeth were serrated for slicing and sawing, rather than curved for snaring. With all of those heads and its poisonous fumes, its victims usually weren't getting away.

SVARA

(s-VAR-ah)

One Deadly Dragon

Armenian folklore tells of a massive yellow dragon so huge that its teeth were as big as a man's arm. It had a colossal horn and large ears. The dragon's name? Svara. It was so deadly that people believed it could poison anything it came into contact with. That's why everyone kept their distance.

Region: Eastern Europe
Time Period: Unknown
Habitat: Unknown
Flight Capable: Unknown
Fire Breath: Unknown

Not much is known about Svara, except that a great hero named Keresapa was able to vanquish it.

Dragon Bite Note #12:

Svara's teeth were about 2 feet (0.6 meters) long. They were pointed at the tip and serrated—or jagged—along the sides for easy slicing.

AMARU

(ah-MAR-oo)

Above and Below

A massive two-headed serpent-like creature that lived underground, Amaru also had wings and feet like a bird's—so it could crawl out from the depths and take to the sky. It was an important part of Incan mythology, and Incans believed that Amaru could move between the real world and the spiritual one. It was also believed to bring rain and out-of-this-world events.

Region: Peru
Time Period: 13th century
Habitat: Underground caves
Flight Capable: Yes
Fire Breath: No

Incans believed Amaru could create rainbows. They thought that one of Amaru's heads would sip in water from a spring and then spit a stream into the air to land in the mouth of its other head. The water's arc was a rainbow.

Dragon Bite Note #13:

Amaru was a two-headed beast. One head looked like a llama's. The other resembled a puma's and was filled with smooth hooked fangs.

PAKHANGBA

(pock-HAWNG-bah)

The Unknown Dragon

A mix between a serpent and a deer with large antlers, Pakhangba lived near the sacred ponds and woodland groves of northeastern India. Not much is known about this unique creature, though some think it offered protection to special places.

Region: India
Time Period: Unknown
Habitat: Mountains and caves, as well as lakes
Flight Capable: Yes
Fire Breath: No

Pakhangba's deer antlers may symbolize gentleness and kindness, as they do in many traditions.

Dragon Bite Note #14:

Pakhangba is often pictured coiled with its own tail in its mouth—clamped between four pointy and curved fangs in its upper and lower jaws.

COCKATRICE

(cock-ah-TREESE)

The Cockatrice was said to be so deadly, a creature could die just by looking at it.

Poison Blood and a Deadly Stare

What happens when an old chicken's egg is cared for and then hatched by a serpent? According to legend, a Cockatrice is born. A mix of dragon, rooster, and serpent, the Cockatrice had a long list of dangerous features. Its mere presence could kill an orchard of fruit trees, and it could poison a lake for centuries just by drinking from it.

Region: North Africa
Time Period: 14th century
Habitat: Deserts
Flight Capable: Yes
Fire Breath: Unknown

Dragon Bite Note #15:

This horrible hybrid had the beak of its chicken ancestors. Like a bird of prey, it had a tomial tooth—a hooked beak—that it stabbed down into its victims.

CHIMERA

(kiy-MER-ah)

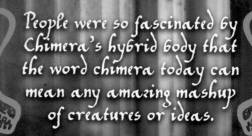

People were so fascinated by Chimera's hybrid body that the word chimera today can mean any amazing mashup of creatures or ideas.

A Monster Mashup

Part dragon, part lion, and part goat, the Chimera is a scary hybrid creature. Chimera was Hydra's sister, and like Hydra, she terrorized the people of ancient Greece. A hero named Bellerophon was only able to beat her with the help of Pegasus, the winged horse.

Region: Southern Europe (Greece)
Time Period: 8th–6th century BC
Habitat: Waterways, like rivers and lakes
Flight Capable: Yes
Fire Breath: Unknown

Dragon Bite Note #16:
Chimera had a variety of teeth, of course. Particularly useful were her lion's fangs and her serrated dragon's teeth.

LINDWORM

(LIND-werm)

Creepy Crawler

With red glowing eyes, a head like a horse's, and the body of a huge serpent, the Lindworm is a spooky creature for sure. In some old Norse and Scandinavian stories, these wingless dragons crept around cemeteries and burial sites, guarding the dead.

Region: Scandinavia
Time Period: Up to the mid-19th century
Habitat: Burial sites
Flight Capable: No
Fire Breath: No

Lindworm sightings were reported all around Scandinavia—in Norway, Sweden, Finland, and Denmark. Sometimes, Lindworms have been reported at sea.

Dragon Bite Note #17:
The Lindworm had an enormous mouth and was able to unhinge its jaws and swallowed its prey whole, like a boa constrictor.

Y DDRAIG GOCH

Welsh Dragon (E DRAYG GOOTCH)

The Red Dragon

According to legend, a king was attempting to build a new castle on a hill, but every night an earthquake toppled any construction done that day. Two dragons were trapped underground battling each other and shaking the earth. The eventual victor was Y Ddraig Goch, the red Welsh dragon.

Region: Britain
Time Period: Early 9th century
Habitat: Underground caves
Flight Capable: Yes
Fire Breath: Yes

Today, y Ddraig Goch is the symbol of Wales, and you can see depictions of it all over the area.

Dragon Bite Note #18:

Y Ddraig Goch had a mouthful of serrated teeth. It also used the horn on its nose to pierce prey and enemies. Its tooth inspired the one that comes with this book.

ZILANT

(zeye-LANT)

Some legends say that Zilant wasn't one being, but was instead made up of hundreds of snakes linked together in the shape of a dragon.

King of the Serpents

Legend has it that people in a small Russian village lived near a pit writhing with big, venomous snakes. One day, they decided to take care of the snakes by setting the snake pit on fire and Zilant rose from the ashes. The king of the serpents, this dragon stood for wisdom and became the symbol of the Russian city of Kazan.

Region: Russia
Time Period: 13th to 16th century
Habitat: Hillsides
Flight Capable: Yes
Fire Breath: Unknown

Dragon Bite Note #19:
Zilant's teeth were thin and needle-like, much like a sand tiger shark's—perfect for snagging slippery prey.

TARASQUE

(teh-RASK)

In some legends, the Tarasque even had a turtle shell complete with spikes, as well as a scorpion's tail.

Total Terror

Picture a dragon's head on the body of an ox, with the feet of a bear. That's the terrible Tarasque, which hailed from southern Europe. Though most reports of the Tarasque came from southern France, it was also known as the Tarasca in southern Spain. This wicked beast preyed on villages until it was tamed and sent away by a saint.

Region: Southern Europe
Time Period: Mid-13th century or before
Habitat: Riverbanks
Flight Capable: No
Fire Breath: Unknown

Dragon Bite Note #20:

Tarasque's triangular and jagged teeth were small, but its top fangs and front claws were deadly.

DRAGONS TODAY

Though they may not be of the fire-breathing type, dragons exist all over the world today! Here are just a few—and the traits they have in common with mythical dragons.

Komodo Dragons

These 10-foot-long (3-meter-long) giant lizards are the biggest lizards in the world. They're top predators built for hunting: They have razor-sharp teeth, claws made for ripping, keen tracking senses, and powerful muscles.

Dragon similarities:

Serpent-like body; four legs equipped with powerful claws; deadly bite

Flying Dragon

These little lizards have flaps of skin along their sides that they can expand. All it takes is a running jump from a tree branch and opening those flaps, to make these lizards airborne!

Dragon similarities: Flying reptiles

Leafy Seadragons

Colorful and wildly camouflaged, Leafy Seadragons blend in with seaweed and float with the tides. They're not the best swimmers, but that's okay—they don't really need to go anywhere, as they suck in nutrients from seawater.

Dragon similarities: Dragon-like heads

Dragonsnakes

Also known as Javan mudsnakes, these 2-foot-long (0.6-meter-long) snakes live in Indonesia. They eat mostly frogs.

Dragon similarities: Scales, mysterious nature

If you have questions or comments about this product,
please visit www.beckermayer.com/customerservice and click on Customer Service Request Form.

becker&mayer!
BOOK PRODUCERS

Sink Your Teeth Into Dragons is produced by becker&mayer! LLC
11120 NE 33rd Place, Suite 101
Bellevue, WA 98004
www.beckermayer.com

Author: L. J. Tracosas
Designer: Sam Dawson
Illustrators: RJ Palmer, and Kerem Beyit
Editor: Paul Ruditis
Photo Researcher: Farley Bookout
Product Developer: Peter Schumacher
Product Sourcing: Jen Matasich
Production coordinator: Tom Miller

ISBN: 978-1-60380-393-9

Project number: 16188

Printed in Shenzhen, China